ABOUT THE AUTHOR

Lois Keith uses a wheelchair. She does a lot of different jobs. She writes, teaches English part-time in a secondary school, gives lectures and runs writing workshops. She has written books that are used for teaching English in schools and has also written many books and articles about disability.

These include an award-winning collection of writing by disabled women called *Mustn't Grumble* and a novel for teenagers called *A Different Life*, about a girl who starts a different life when she begins to use a wheelchair.

Lois lives in London with her husband and her two teenage daughters. Their house is specially designed to include someone who uses a wheelchair.

Contents

4   People who use wheelchairs

6   Why can't some people walk?

8   A history of wheelchair users

10   Schools of the past

12   Schools today

14   At home

16   Out and about

18   Around the world

20   Sport

22   Fun and games

24   Going to work

26   Being a success

28   Looking to the future

30   Glossary and useful addresses

32   Index

People who use wheelchairs

There are many different reasons why people use wheelchairs. Some people can walk a little but use a wheelchair if they have a long way to go. Some people's legs don't work at all so they have to use a wheelchair all the time. Their wheelchair is like a pair of legs. It is their way of getting around.

Look around you

Do you know anyone who uses a wheelchair? If you go to a place such as a modern shopping centre, where everything is on one level or where there are lifts to use, you will see many people who use wheelchairs. But in places where there are uneven surfaces, stairs or kerbs without **ramps**, you may not see anyone using a wheelchair.

Sets of wheels

Choosing the right wheelchair is like buying a new pair of shoes. You need to find a pair that fits you just right. Someone who cannot walk needs a wheelchair that is the right fit for them. If the wheelchair is too big or too small, too heavy or too light it will be much more difficult to use.

▶ **Many big shopping centres now have lifts as well as moving staircases.**

think about
BEING IN A
WHEELCHAIR

Lois Keith

Chrysalis Children's Books

First published in the UK in 1998 by
Chrysalis Children's Books
An imprint of Chrysalis Books Group PLC
The Chrysalis Building, Bramley Road, London W10 6SP

Paperback edition first published in 2004

ISBN 1 85561 806 0 (hb)
ISBN 1 84138 791 6 (pb)
British Library Cataloguing in Publication Data for this book
is available from the British Library.

Printed in Hong Kong
10 9 8 7 6 5 4 3 2 (hb)
10 9 8 7 6 5 4 3 2 1 (pb)

Editor: Stephanie Bellwood
Designer: Guy Callaby
Picture researcher: Kathy Lockley
Illustrator: Richard Prideaux
Consultant: Elizabeth Atkinson
Series consultant: Peter White, BBC Disability Affairs Correspondent

To Colin, Rachel and Miriam

Picture acknowledgements:
Allsport: 21t Clive Brunskill, 20b Todd Warshaw. Breckenridge & Viana: 15b. Collections:
29b Anthea Sieveking, cover Brian Shuel, 4b Roger Scruton. Corbis-Bettmann/UPI: 26b.
Disability Now: 5t, 7t, 21b, 25tr John Grooms Association, 29t. Louise Dyson Agency: 24b.
Mary Evans Picture Library: 9t. Format Partners: 16cr Brenda Prince, 14b & 17t Joanne
O'Brien, 13t & 28b Ulrike Preuss. Gisele Freund/Agence Nina Beskow: 27tr. Getty Images:
10t, 6t Andrea Booher, 8t Ken Fisher, 18t Yaun Layma. Hugo Glendinning/CandoCo Dance
Company: 23cr. Ronald Grant Archive: 9b Warner Bros., 1993. Sally & Richard Greenhill: 7b,
12b, 15t, 22t, 22b. Robert Harding Picture Library: 12t, 16tl. Hulton Getty: 8b. Image Bank:
14t L.D. Gordon. Long & Stebbens: 17b. London Metropolitan Archive: 10b, 11t. Mattel UK
Ltd: 23tl. Motivation/David Constantine: 18b, 19b, 19t. Photofusion: 13b David Tothill.
Pictor: 4t, 28t, 20t & 24t Uniphoto. Quest Enabling Designs Ltd: 5b. Redferns: 27bl Leon
Morris. Rex Features: 26t Sipa Press, 27c Tim Rooke. Colin Schofield: 3t. Lord Mayor Treloar
Archive, North Hampshire Hospitals NHS Trust: 11b.

Words in **bold** are explained in the glossary on pages 30 and 31.

Types of wheelchairs

There are many kinds of wheelchairs. A chair that people push themselves by turning the wheels is called a manual wheelchair. Some people prefer electric wheelchairs or scooters. Electric wheelchairs are sturdy and strong and work by pushing a button on the arm of the chair. They are called electric but they really work by battery. Other people have light, sporty wheelchairs that are easy to fold up and put in a car. People who use this kind of wheelchair usually have strong arms.

Some people need help with pushing their chair, but most people who use wheelchairs prefer to get around independently, even if they have someone with them.

This wheelchair is designed for children. The seat moves up or down so children can sit at the same table as their friends, reach high shelves or pick up something from the floor.

THINK ABOUT

Getting around

If you used a wheelchair, could you get into your home? Would you be able to go into your classroom at school or out into the playground with your friends? Most people who use wheelchairs can get around very well where the pavement or the floor is flat and smooth. Staircases are difficult or impossible for wheelchair users, but if there is a lift, they can manage just as well as anyone else.

Why can't some people walk?

There are many reasons why people have difficulties walking. Some people are born with a condition which affects the way they move. Other people have an accident or an illness as they are growing up or when they are older.

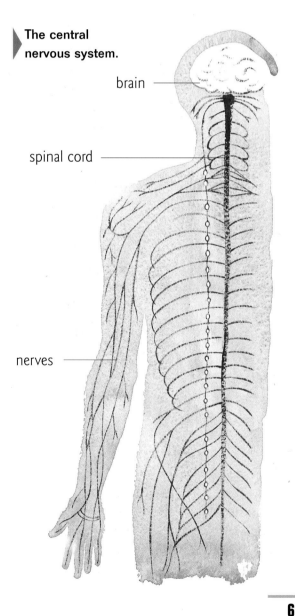

▶ The central nervous system.

brain

spinal cord

nerves

The spinal cord

If you put your fingers on the back of your neck you will feel some hard bits that stick out and run right down your back. These are bony rings called **vertebrae**. They protect your **spinal cord** which is soft and bendy. Your spinal cord contains millions of **nerves** that send messages from your brain to all the different parts of your body. For example, if you want to wiggle your toes, your brain sends the message through your spinal cord, along your nerves, down your legs to your feet. When the message reaches the muscles in your toes they can wiggle.

Damage to the spinal cord

A person's spinal cord can be damaged in an accident or by a condition such as **spina bifida** or **multiple sclerosis**. If this happens, messages cannot be sent properly from the brain to parts of the body. This means that these parts of the body can become **paralysed**.

Other wheelchair users

Some people who use wheelchairs have conditions that affect the control of their muscles such as **muscular dystrophy** or **cerebral palsy**. Some people have **brittle bones** that break easily and do not grow properly. Some people have **arthritis** that makes their **joints** painful and stiff.

These are just a few of the reasons why some people use wheelchairs. But whatever the reason, a wheelchair is not a prison. It is an important piece of equipment that gives people who have difficulty walking the freedom to go where they want.

▲ Tanni Grey is a famous athlete. She was born with spina bifida and has used a wheelchair since she was seven. Tanni has won Paralympic gold medals for wheelchair racing, and she has won the London Marathon twice.

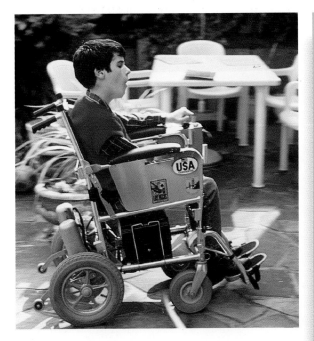

▲ This boy has cerebral palsy. People with cerebral palsy may have trouble using their arms or their legs.

THINK ABOUT

Health

Most people who use wheelchairs aren't ill. Part of their body doesn't work properly but they are still active and well. Some people use a wheelchair all their lives. Some use them for a short time, perhaps because they are recovering from an operation or have broken their leg while playing a sport.

A history of wheelchair users

When you imagine someone who uses a wheelchair, do you think of someone young or someone old? In the first half of the twentieth century most physically disabled people in Britain were younger than 14, but now most people in a wheelchair are older. This is because childhood illnesses are easier to prevent nowadays. Older people are more likely to need a wheelchair because their bodies don't work as well as they used to.

Poverty and disease

In the past, children often became disabled because they were poor. Children who lived in houses with no proper toilets or clean water were very unhealthy. They often caught diseases that stopped their bodies from growing properly. Children who did not have enough healthy food to eat often had **rickets**, which made their legs thin and weak. Thousands of children in the first half of this century had a disease called **polio**. Many of them died or became disabled. Doctors were expensive, so if a child became ill or had an accident, their parents could not afford medical treatment and the child's body would not heal properly.

▶ **This photograph of poor Hungarian children was taken in 1920. The girl is suffering from rickets. Even now there are many parts of the world where children do not have enough good food to eat or do not see a doctor regularly.**

A wheelchair of your own

Finding a good wheelchair was a problem for many people who couldn't walk. Wheelchairs were very expensive and most families could not afford them. Poorer parents often made their own using scrap materials so that their disabled child could move around more.

This wheelchair was sold in London in 1844.

Children in stories

Many famous children's books tell stories about disabled people who are magically cured. In the book *Heidi*, a disabled girl called Clara is suddenly able to walk, so she doesn't have to depend on other people any more. In the past, people often believed that you could not be independent or active if you used a wheelchair.

THINK ABOUT

Superstition

In the past there was a lot of ignorance, fear and superstition about disabled people. They were called horrible names such as cripples or physical defectives. Some people believed that having a disabled child was a punishment for bad things the family had done, and that the child was possessed by the devil. Disabled children were very frightened by these attitudes. Things are better today, but sometimes disabled people are presented in a negative way. This can make children feel frightened of people who use wheelchairs, and it does not help disabled people feel good about themselves.

This is a scene from a film of *The Secret Garden*. The story is about a boy called Colin who has spent most of his life in bed. He is furious when someone calls him a 'poor crippled boy', so he pushes his wheelchair away and walks. In real life there are few miraculous cures for people who cannot walk.

Schools of the past

In the first half of this century, many disabled children did not go to school. There was a lot of fear and **prejudice** about disabled children. Some headteachers refused to teach them because they thought that the way disabled children looked might frighten the other children.

▶ If disabled children were sent to school at all they often did not have a good education. The boys at this school had to make their own chairs to sit on.

Staying at home

Disabled children often had to stay at home instead of going to school. This was very upsetting for children who were desperate to learn to read and write and play with their friends. They would see their brothers and sisters going to school and feel very left out.

Some disabled children went to primary school but were not allowed to go on to secondary school. Parents tried to help their children to learn, but it wasn't the same. A few teachers did try to include disabled children in school life, but this did not happen very often.

Special schools

Some children who couldn't walk were sent to special schools. These were often called Cripples Schools. The children did a few sums and a little bit of reading and spent most of the time sewing or making simple things. This could be very boring. Children who were sent to these schools often wished that they could go to ordinary schools. They did not want to feel left out and different from other children.

Children of all ages at special schools were given the same simple lessons. Some people believed that because a child had difficulty walking, they were not able to understand.

Many people believed that plenty of fresh air would help to cure disabled children. Lessons were often given outside.

Sent away to school

Children were sometimes as young as three years old when they were sent away to a special school. The school could be a long way from home and often parents were only allowed to visit once a year. Families who were very poor couldn't afford to visit at all. Special schools could be cruel places. Children often had their hair cut short and wore a uniform with a number on it. If the teachers and nurses wanted to see a child, they called out their number instead of their name. This made children unhappy and lonely.

THINK ABOUT

Types of schools

Some people think that it is better for children who use wheelchairs to go to school with all the other children who use wheelchairs. Other people believe that all children should be able to go to their local school with their friends and their brothers and sisters. What do you think?

Schools today

If someone who uses a wheelchair came to your school what would have to be changed so that they could join in everything? Think how they would get around the building, use the toilets, or go into the playground. What changes would you make to your school so that everyone could be included?

Designing a school

Some new schools are specially designed to include disabled pupils, including children who use wheelchairs. Often the school is all on one floor with smooth, even surfaces that are easier to wheel around on. There are **adapted** toilets and sometimes there is an area where people in wheelchairs can go if they want to be quiet or need to do special exercises.

Pupils who use wheelchairs can join in every part of school life. Some things might need to be changed slightly. For example, the height of the tables could be altered so that wheelchairs could fit under them.

◀ **This classroom has an adjustable table. It has been fixed at just the right level for this boy to work at.**

School buildings

How old is your school? Some school buildings were built more than a hundred years ago. At this time people did not think about including children who used wheelchairs, so these buildings often have lots of stairs. But everyone can be included if a few changes are made. Ramps can be fitted if there are just a few stairs. Some schools have new classrooms added on to the ground floor, and some schools have a lift installed.

▶ This school has a ramp as well as stairs attached to an outdoor classroom.

▲ These boys enjoy playing football in games lessons at their London school. What is your favourite activity at school?

Extra activities

It isn't too hard to include everyone in school activities. It just takes a little thought and planning. Think of a school trip you have been on. How do you think someone in your class who used a wheelchair would have managed? And what kinds of activities could they take part in on sports day? They could easily join in your games lessons too.

THINK ABOUT

In the playground

What games do you like to play in the playground? Could someone who uses a wheelchair play too? You might only have to change the game a bit to let them join in. Someone in a wheelchair could easily join in a game of tig or chase. If your playground surface is smooth, they might move faster than you can run! If you lowered the netball or basketball pole they could join in these games too.

At home

If someone in your home used a wheelchair, how would they manage? Would they be able to get into all the rooms by themselves? People who use wheelchairs like to have a lot of space to get around so you might have to be a bit tidier! Leaving a pair of boots or your school bag in the middle of the room could be very annoying.

Around the house

People who use wheelchairs need to be able to get into all the rooms used by the family. Flats, apartments and bungalows are usually all on one level, but there are ways to **adapt** a house that has stairs. **Ramps** can be built in places where there are just a few stairs, such as steps outside leading to the front door.

This woman has had her front pathway specially designed so that it is a gentle slope rather than steps. This means that she can go in and out of her house easily. Slopes are also useful for people pushing a pram, riding a bicycle or roller skating.

The right height

Think how annoying it can be when things are at the wrong height for you, such as a shelf that is too high to reach. The height of things is very important to wheelchair users. Toilets for disabled people are often higher. In the kitchen it is easier for someone in a wheelchair to cook and prepare food if the work surfaces and the cooker are lower than usual. Sockets for plugs should be in the middle of the wall rather than near the floor.

Children who use wheelchairs can do the same things at home as you, as long as everything is in the right place and at the right height. This boy enjoys playing with his friend.

This is a special lift that can be used at home to go upstairs or downstairs.

Home equipment

Many ordinary things at home can be adapted for a wheelchair user. It is easier for someone in a wheelchair to find something in a drawer that pulls out rather than having to reach into deep cupboards. There is also a lot of special equipment for people who use wheelchairs. In the bathroom, some people use a fold-down shower seat so that they can move from their wheelchair into the shower.

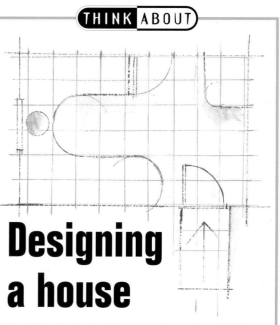

THINK ABOUT

Designing a house

Families include all sorts of people: children, older people, and people who are disabled. Architects are beginning to think about this when they build new homes. For example, many new homes are now built with wider doors and corridors to help people in wheelchairs to move around. How would you design a new house so that someone who uses a wheelchair could live there?

Out and about

People who use wheelchairs like to go out and about just like everyone else. They need flat surfaces to help them get around easily. Anything that has wheels needs a flat surface. When you ride a bike or go roller skating you move along much faster if the path is smooth.

▼ This mother has a baby seat attached to the front of her wheelchair. It helps her to go out with her children more easily.

Playgrounds

Does your local park have an adventure playground? Could any of the equipment be used by children who use wheelchairs? Some disabled children can get out of their wheelchairs to play on the roundabout or climbing frame, but for others this is difficult. Perhaps you could think about how to redesign some playground equipment so that a friend with a wheelchair could join in the fun.

(THINK ABOUT)

Helping people

Imagine that you are trying to lift a heavy box. It is very nice if someone offers to help you carry it. But if you are managing on your own, it is very annoying if they pull the box out of your hands and carry it themselves. Sometimes people don't know whether they should ask disabled people if they would like help. The trick is just to look and see. When you think you could do something helpful for a person who uses a wheelchair, just ask them if they would like some help. If they don't need it, they will just say 'No thank you'.

Older buildings

In the past, disabled people were not expected to go out and about much, so most older buildings were not designed to include wheelchair users. But by adding things such as **ramps** or lifts, buildings can be **adapted** so that everyone can use them.

▲ **This building has been made accessible to wheelchair users by having a ramp.**

Public transport

It is often impossible for people who use wheelchairs to travel by bus or train, or on underground railways. There are lots of steps and narrow doors to squeeze through. This makes disabled people angry because public transport is often the only way to get out and about if they don't have a car.

Driving

Many adults who use wheelchairs drive their own car. They have special hand controls rather than foot pedals. Some disabled drivers fold up their wheelchair and put it on another seat before driving off. Some vans are adapted so that the person can drive in their wheelchair. Some cars have a device that lifts the wheelchair on to the roof and stores it in a roof box while the person is driving.

This van is adapted for wheelchair users. The driver wheels on to a tail lift that rises to the van's floor level. The driver moves into the driving position, and the doors close by remote control.

Around the world

There may be as many as 20 million people around the world who need a wheelchair but who can't afford one. Most of these people live in **developing countries**. Wheelchairs are expensive and hard to find in these parts of the world. This makes life very difficult for people who can't walk easily.

This man lost both his legs in a landmine blast in Afghanistan. He uses a special three-wheeled chair, and turns hand pedals to move the wheelchair forwards.

Making wheelchairs

A charity called Motivation trains people in developing countries to design and make their own wheelchairs. The designs need to be cheap and made with materials that local people can find easily.

The Motivation team has to think carefully about the design of different wheelchairs. In countries such as Cambodia, it is difficult to find the steel tubes usually needed to make wheelchairs, so the Motivation workers have designed a wheelchair made out of wood. In other countries such as Bangladesh, the roads can be very uneven so the wheelchairs need extra large, strong wheels.

The right wheelchair

In poor countries, disabled children often have wheelchairs **donated** to them by richer countries. These wheelchairs are heavy, old and much too big for children. Giving a child a wheelchair that is the wrong size is like giving you a huge pair of shoes and then telling you to run as fast as you can! Motivation makes wheelchairs that suit the age and needs of each person.

The Moti

A wheelchair has to last a long time in poor countries, so it is important that it can change as the child grows. Motivation has designed a chair for children called the Moti. It is light, comfortable, and suits children of all ages and levels of disability. The Moti lets many children sit up, move around and play for the first time.

These Indonesian men have been trained by the Motivation team to make wheelchairs.

This Russian boy has cerebral palsy. He was carried everywhere before he had a Moti wheelchair. Now he can sit up and look around him. The chair will be adjusted as he grows.

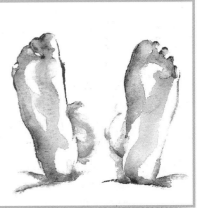

THINK ABOUT

Missing out

In some parts of the world it is difficult or impossible to find wheelchairs for children who need them. These children have to stay at home or lie in bed all day. If they have a condition such as cerebral palsy their balance might not be good enough to sit up on their own. They need a good wheelchair so that they can sit up and look around them. Without a wheelchair it is hard for these children to learn about the world around them.

Sport

Some people who use wheelchairs are very adventurous. They like to go horse-riding, water-skiing, sailing, scuba diving, abseiling down cliffs and even bungee jumping! Wheelchair users can take part in just about any sport. They might need help with some activities, but they can manage many others independently.

▶ Basketball is one of the events in the Paralympic Games. This event takes place at the same time as the Olympic Games. The Paralympics are for all disabled people, and there are many events that include wheelchair athletes.

Basketball

Basketball is the most organized wheelchair sport. It has been played for over 50 years. Wheelchair basketball started after the Second World War as an activity for fit young men who had been disabled fighting in the war.

The first teams had names such as California Flying Wheels, Rolling Pioneers and New Jersey Wheelers. Wheelchair basketball is now played by men and women all over the world. It is exciting to watch because it is a very fast game.

Skiing

There are many different ways that people who have difficulty walking can be helped to ski. A ski-bob is a single ski with a lightweight, plastic seat attached for the skier to sit on. The skier uses their hands to help balance the ski-bob as they race downhill. Some people use a ski-kart. This looks a bit like a sledge. The skier uses hand controls to steer it.

A ski-bob competition in the Winter Paralympics.

Wheelchair racing

If you have ever watched a marathon race you will probably have seen the wheelchair racers. Wheelchairs built for racing are very lightweight and strong. Each chair is specially designed to suit the individual racer.

Wheelchair athletes train hard. They swim, work out in the gym and can wheel 32 kilometres or more each day.

THINK ABOUT

Your favourite sport

What kind of sports do you like? Do you like to play team games such as cricket or rounders, or do you prefer activities such as canoeing, rock climbing or horse-riding? Choose one activity and work out a way that a friend who uses a wheelchair could join in.

Fun and games

People who use wheelchairs like to have fun just like everyone else. Not everyone is sporty but whatever is going on, disabled people would rather join in than watch. What do you like to do? Perhaps you like watching television, playing on the computer, dancing, reading or playing football. These are all things that disabled children like to do too!

This hoist makes getting into a swimming pool easy. The helper is turning a handle that lowers the swimmer into the water.

Swimming pools

Have a look around your local swimming pool. Are there any **facilities** for wheelchair users, such as a changing room with lots of space? Some disabled people can go to a swimming pool on their own but there are also things designed to help. Some pools have a hoist.

Wheelchair users move from their wheelchair into another seat that is lowered into the water. Modern pools often have a gentle slope into the water instead of steps. Disabled people can borrow a special waterproof wheelchair and wheel straight into the water.

All kinds of toys

Every child is different. Some are tall, some are small. Some are black, some are white. Some love football, others like to draw pictures. Some children walk, others use wheelchairs. Nowadays there are toys that reflect some of these differences. The company that makes Barbie Dolls also makes a doll called Share a Smile Becky who uses a wheelchair. Unfortunately they didn't alter the Barbie house, so Becky couldn't get through her own front door!

Share a Smile Becky talks to her Barbie doll friends.

Dance

Wheelchairs can move very fast in all sorts of ways and some people who use wheelchairs love to dance. CandoCo is a dance company that has disabled and non-disabled dancers. The wheelchairs are part of the dance. They spin around, tip back and are lifted into the air. The dancers move their arms and their bodies.

The CandoCo dance group travels all round the world to perform shows and run dance classes.

THINK ABOUT

Holidays

Everyone likes to go on holiday. Some people like restful holidays where they sit on the beach all day. Other people prefer adventure holidays. Caravans and even tents can be adapted for wheelchairs. This is great for children and adults who use wheelchairs and like active, outdoor holidays.

Going to work

Although disabled people have many talents and skills, it is not always easy for them to find work and show what they can do. Some people find it hard to imagine that a disabled person can do a job as well as someone else. There are also employers who are not willing to **adapt** their workplace so that someone in a wheelchair could get around. But when wheelchair users are given the chance, there are very few jobs that they cannot do.

Working lives

The Second World War changed the working lives of many disabled people in Britain. As fit young men were called up into the army, navy and air force, there was a desperate need for workers at home. Disabled men and women were given jobs in factories, hospitals, offices and on farms. It was the first time that many disabled people had been able to work.

Here are a few modern examples of people who use wheelchairs and the jobs they have. Would you like to do any of these things?

Shannon Murray is a model. In 1994 she won a modelling competition and now her work takes her all over the world.

Mik Scarlet is a musician and television presenter. Mik abseiled down a building as part of a campaign to make people aware of all the things disabled people can do.

Jane's teachers never thought that she would have a job when she grew up. Now she works hard to make sure that disabled people are given a fair chance at school and at work.

Campaigning

Jane Campbell is a wheelchair user who **campaigns** for equal rights for disabled people. She runs an organization that helps disabled people to live independently in their own homes. Equal rights are very important to Jane. When she was young she was sent to a special school. She missed her friends and wanted to go to the local school so much that she made her mum buy her the uniform, even though she didn't go there!

THINK ABOUT

Careers

What kind of job would you like to do when you leave school? Perhaps you are good at art and want to be an illustrator or designer, or maybe you would like a glamorous job such as being a singer or an actor. Or perhaps you want to train to be a teacher, a doctor or a lawyer. People who use wheelchairs do all these jobs.

Being a success

Sometimes people imagine that wheelchair users sit around all day waiting for someone to come along and help them. They would be surprised if they knew how much people who use wheelchairs can achieve. There have been many famous wheelchair users through history. As attitudes change and disabled people are given a chance to show what they can do, more and more people who use wheelchairs will be remembered for their talents and achievements.

Franklin D Roosevelt (1882-1945)

Franklin D Roosevelt was the longest serving American president and also one of the most admired. In 1921 he caught **polio** which **paralysed** his legs. Roosevelt was elected president in 1933. Many people thought that a disabled person couldn't do such an important job, but President Roosevelt helped to make America financially successful and led his country through the Second World War. He also set up an international centre for the study and treatment of polio.

◀ **Franklin D Roosevelt hardly ever appeared in public in his wheelchair. Thousands of photographs of him were taken, but only two show him in a wheelchair. Here he is wearing callipers to support his legs.**

Frida Kahlo (1907-1954)

Frida Kahlo was a Mexican painter. She married another famous artist called Diego Rivera. She loved to use bright colours in her paintings and many of them are self-portraits. She often wore traditional Mexican dress with long skirts, shawls and bright headdresses. When Frida Kahlo was 18 years old she was involved in a very bad road accident and spent a lot of time in hospital. Many of her paintings show her feelings about being ill and in pain.

▲ Frida Kahlo with her doctor. Her painting shows herself with a portrait of the doctor.

Itzhak Perlman (born 1945)

Itzhak Perlman is a world-famous violinist. He was born in Israel and moved to America when he was 13 to study classical music. He has made many recordings of his music and appears in concerts all over the world. He had polio when he was young, and now uses a wheelchair. He is a strong believer in equal rights for disabled people.

▲ Stephen Hawking travels all over the world to give talks about his scientific theories.

Stephen Hawking (born 1942)

Stephen Hawking is a **physicist** and one of the most brilliant scientists of the twentieth century. He is a professor at Cambridge University and has written many scientific books. His most famous book is called *A Brief History of Time*. He uses a wheelchair because he has a condition called **motor neurone disease**. This condition has also affected his voice so he speaks through a computer.

◀ Itzhak Perlman playing in a classical concert.

THINK ABOUT

Finding out more

Try and find out more about the people on this page, or about any other famous people you've heard of who use wheelchairs.

Looking to the future

Imagine being invited to a party but being told when you arrive that you can't come in. You would feel very left out. This is how someone in a wheelchair feels when they go to a place that is not **accessible** to them. They might be told that they can't get in because the building has stairs, or because it would be too dangerous. This makes disabled people angry and upset.

These friends go to a play centre together.
One of the children is celebrating his birthday.

Changing laws

All over the world disabled people and their friends and families **campaign** to make sure that everyone has the right to be included. Children who use wheelchairs should be able to go to the school where their brothers, sisters and friends go if that is the right school for them. People should be able to get into public buildings such as libraries and cinemas. They should be able to travel on buses and trains. They should have the chance to go to colleges or universities and to get good jobs.

Medical help

In the last hundred years there have been many developments to help people who can't walk. There is now a **vaccine** to prevent **polio**, and **antibiotics** can cure many diseases. People who have lost limbs can have **artificial** ones that work nearly as well as real limbs. There are operations to replace worn-out **joints** with metal ones.

What does the future hold?

Scientists are working to develop electrical devices that **bypass** a damaged **spinal cord** and can make **paralysed** muscles move better. They are also trying to find cures for all kinds of diseases. But many disabled people do not believe that a cure is the most important thing. They are much more interested in having the same rights as everyone else and the same freedom to move around.

A mother who uses a wheelchair reads a book with her young daughter.

A campaign to improve public transport. In some cities all buses have a platform that lowers to let wheelchair users roll straight on to the bus. This is also useful for parents with babies in prams or pushchairs.

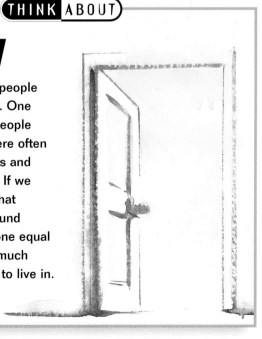

THINK ABOUT

Equality

There will always be people who use wheelchairs. One hundred years ago, people who couldn't walk were often kept away from others and hardly ever went out. If we design buildings so that everyone can get around them and give everyone equal chances, it will be a much fairer world for us all to live in.

Glossary

accessible   Easy to enter or use. Buildings that are accessible for wheelchair users might have lifts or ramps, and plenty of space inside to move around.

adapted   Changed or improved. If a building is adapted for people who use wheelchairs, it might have wide doors and corridors.

antibiotic   A medicine that can cure diseases or stop them becoming any worse. An example of an antibiotic is penicillin.

arthritis   A painful illness that causes swollen and stiff joints. If a person has arthritis in their leg joints they might find walking very difficult.

artificial   Something that is specially made, not natural.

brittle bones   Bones that crack or break easily because they have not grown strong enough. Some people have weak, brittle bones because they have not eaten enough healthy food containing vitamins needed for growth.

bypass   To miss out or avoid. Devices are being developed for people with spinal injuries which doctors hope will trigger nerve messages themselves, bypassing the spinal cord.

campaign   To work to change something such as a law or a way of thinking. People can campaign by giving speeches, writing books, letters or articles, or having marches and demonstrations.

cerebral palsy   A condition that some people are born with or develop just after birth. People with cerebral palsy may have trouble using their arms and legs. Some might use a wheelchair, and some people may need help communicating.

developing countries
Poor countries that are trying to improve their farming, factories, health and so on.

donated   To have given something away, usually to a charity or to someone in need.

facilities   Special equipment or an adapted area to make things easier for people. One facility for people who use wheelchairs is a wide telephone booth with a telephone that is lower than usual.

joints   Places in the body where two bones are linked, or jointed, so that each bone can move freely. An example of a joint is the knee, which connects two large leg bones.

motor neurone disease
Motor nerves are nerves that carry messages to muscles to make them move. Motor neurone disease stops these nerves from working properly. This means that muscles become very weak.

multiple sclerosis   A disease of the brain, the spinal cord and the nerves. This affects muscles and can sometimes paralyse limbs. Multiple sclerosis might also affect a person's sight and speech.

muscular dystrophy
A disease that causes muscles to become weaker, so that the person cannot walk very well.

nerves   Tiny, thin threads that carry messages to and from the brain. There are nerves in all parts of the body.

paralysed   Having no feeling and not being able to move. If a person's brain, spinal cord or nerves are damaged, then parts of their body might be paralysed.

physicist A person who studies physics. Physics is the scientific study of the world around us.

polio An infectious disease often caught by children. If the infection reaches the spinal cord it can cause muscles to become paralysed. Nowadays children are prevented from catching polio by having a vaccine when they are babies. In poor countries children do not always have this vaccine, and many still catch polio.

prejudice An unfair dislike of a person or a group of people. People can suffer many kinds of prejudice, for example because of their skin colour or because they are disabled.

ramp A sloping floor or path that is built instead of, or as well as, steps. Some ramps can be fitted over steps to make a temporary slope.

rickets A disease that mainly affects children. It happens if children do not eat enough foods containing vitamin D, such as milk and eggs. Rickets cause bones to become soft. Children can also be born with rickets if their mothers did not have healthy food to eat while they were pregnant.

spina bifida This can happen when a baby is growing inside its mother and parts of its spine do not join up properly. A person with spina bifida has difficulty walking and might use braces, crutches or a wheelchair to get around.

spinal cord Part of the body's control centre. The brain passes messages to the spinal cord. Nerves lead from the spinal cord to all parts of the body, and they pass on these messages. This controls everything the body does. The spinal cord is protected by bones called vertebrae.

vaccine A vaccine is a liquid that is injected or swallowed to protect against a disease. It contains a very weak form of the disease which makes the body build up a strong resistance to that disease. If the person then comes into contact with the disease, they will not catch it.

vertebrae The small bones that run from your neck all the way down your back. They protect the sensitive spinal cord and also support the rest of the body. These bones are called the backbone, or the spinal column.

Useful addresses

Here are some addresses you can write to for more information about people who use wheelchairs.

The Back-Up Trust (a charity that helps adults with spinal injuries to take part in challenging outdoor sports)
The Business Village, Broomhill Road, London SW18 4JQ
Please send an S.A.E and postal order for £2.

CandoCo (a dance company of disabled and non-disabled dancers – see page 23)
2L Leroy House, 436 Essex Road, London N1 3QP

Motivation (a charity working in developing countries to make wheelchairs – see pages 18-19)
Brockley Academy, Brockley Lane, Backwell, Bristol BS48 4AQ

The Multiple Sclerosis Society (a charity helping people with multiple sclerosis and their families and friends)
25 Effie Road, London SW6 1EE

Quest Enabling Designs Ltd (QED) (manufacturers of the Bobcat DX – see page 5 – and suppliers of a range of equipment and mobility products)
Ability House, 242 Gosport Road, Fareham, Hampshire PO16 0SS

Scope (the UK's largest charity for people with cerebral palsy, providing services and campaigning for equality)
6 Market Road, London N7 9PW

Spinal Injuries Association (a charity that works for people with spinal injuries, run by people who have spinal injuries themselves)
76 St James's Lane, London N10 3DF

Whizz-Kidz (a charity that raises money to provide all kinds of mobility aids for disabled children)
1 Warwick Row, London SW1E 5ER

Index

accidents 6, 8, 27
antibiotics 29, 30
arthritis 7, 30
artificial limbs 29, 30

basketball 13, 20
brain 6
Brief History of Time, A 27
brittle bones 7, 30

callipers 26
campaigning 25, 28, 30
Campbell, Jane 25
CandoCo 23
caravans 23
cars 17
cerebral palsy 7, 19, 30
Cripples Schools 10, 11

dance 23
developing countries 18, 19, 30
diseases 8, 29

equal rights 25, 27, 28, 29

fear 9, 10
food 8

games 13, 22, 23
Grey, Tanni 7

hand controls 17, 18, 21
Hawking, Stephen 27
Heidi 9
height 12, 15
helping 16
hoist 22
holidays 23
homes 5, 14, 15

ignorance 9

jobs 24, 25, 28
joints 7, 29, 30

Kahlo, Frida 27
kerbs 4
kitchens 15

landmines 18
lifts 4, 5, 13, 15, 17

making wheelchairs 18, 19
marathons 7, 21
miracle cures 9
Motivation 18, 19
motor neurone disease 27, 30
multiple sclerosis 6, 30
Murray, Shannon 24
muscles 6, 7, 29

muscular dystrophy 7, 30

nerves 6, 30

open-air schools 11
operations 7, 29

Paralympic Games 7, 20, 21
paralysis 6, 26, 29, 30
Perlman, Itzhak 27
playgrounds 16
polio 8, 26, 27, 29, 31
poverty 8
prejudice 10, 31
public buildings 4, 17, 22, 28, 29
public transport 17, 28, 29

racing 7, 21
ramps 4, 13, 14, 17, 31
reading 10
rickets 8, 31
Roosevelt, Franklin D 26

Scarlet, Mik 25
school 5, 10, 11, 12, 13, 25, 28
school trips 13
scooters 5

Second World War 20, 24, 26
Secret Garden, The 9
Share a Smile Becky 23
shower seats 15
skiing 21
special schools 10, 11, 25
spina bifida 6, 7, 31
spinal cord 6, 29, 31
sport 7, 20, 21, 22
stairs 4, 5, 12, 14, 28
stories 9
superstition 9
surfaces 4, 5, 12, 13, 14, 16
swimming pools 22

tables 12
tents 23
toilets 12, 15
toys 23

vaccines 29, 31
vertebrae 6, 31

wheelchairs
  adjustable 5, 19
  electric 5
  home-made 9
  manual 5
  Moti 19
  three-wheeled 18
  waterproof 22
  wooden 18